W9-AOX-704

# THE GUARDIAN ANGELS

# James Haskins

ENSLOW PUBLISHERS
Bloy Street and Ramsey Avenue
Box 777
Hillside, New Jersey 07205

**Library of Congress Cataloging in Publication Data:**
Haskins, James, 1941-
    The Guardian Angels.

    Includes index.
    Summary: Traces the development of an organization of
volunteers, dedicated to prevention of crime in the streets and
on subways, founded by New Yorker Curtis Sliwa in 1979.
    1. Guardian Angels (Organization)—Juvenile literature.
2. Sliwa, Curtis, 1954-      —Juvenile literature. 3. Crime prevention—New York—Citizen participation—Biography—Juvenile literature. [1. Guardian Angels (Organization) 2. Sliwa, Curtis,
1954-    . 3. Crime prevention. 4. Social action] I. Title.

HV7431.H38          1983          364.4          82-11615
ISBN 0-89490-081-1

Printed in the United States of America

10 9 8 7 6 5 4 3 2 1

# Contents

# A Good Gang?

They are mostly young, mostly male, and mostly black and Hispanic. They always travel in groups, and they ride the subways and
buses and prowl the most dangerous streets at night. They wear
distinctive colors, and while their mouths are set in straight, grim
lines, their eyes are constantly darting back and forth, up and down,
looking for trouble. A typical gang of young ghetto toughs just
waiting to prey on innocent people? No. Someone who has not heard
of them might think so, but that person would be wrong. This particular gang's policy is to *protect* people. Why else would they call
themselves the Guardian Angels?

Who are the Guardian Angels? In their brief existence, many
people have asked that question. According to the Angels and their
supporters, they are a force for good. They are individuals who have
decided to step in and do something about crime. They say that this
is the only way to recapture the streets from the criminals and give
safe streets back to the citizens.

Some people do not believe these answers. They say that the

Angels are a paramilitary group who have decided to take the law into their own hands. These people think the Angels are more likely to do harm than good. They also charge that the Angels are far less interested in preventing crime than in getting publicity and that this is especially true of the group's founder and director, Curtis Sliwa.

Whoever they are, Curtis Sliwa and the Guardian Angels are one of the most talked-about groups in America. This book tells why.

# The "Arch"angel

Some people seem to be "born leaders"—they are able to inspire other people to follow them. Leadership in itself is neither good nor bad. Leaders can lead other people in bad causes (Hitler, the Reverend Jim Jones), just as they can lead people in good causes (Winston Churchill, the Reverend Martin Luther King, Jr.). When it comes to the qualities of leadership, good or bad reasons for leading are not as important as the ability to lead. Some people have that ability more than others. Curtis Sliwa not only has it, but clearly he has had it from an early age.

Part of the reason may be that Curtis took on family responsibility (or at least thought he did) when he was quite young. He was born in the Canarsie section of Brooklyn, New York, in 1954. His father, Chester, a second-generation Polish-American, was a merchant seaman. That meant that Mr. Sliwa was away from his family and at sea for months at a time. Curtis was the only son, and he took on the care of his mother and two older sisters. Frances Sliwa, his mother, of Italian-American heritage, worked as a dental technician, so Curtis and his sisters were cared for by their grandparents, who were very strict and whom they respected.

It was also at an early age that Curtis learned that he liked getting publicity and being known. He was only six years old when his mother managed to get him on the "Romper Room" television show. Little Curtis was just one of several young children who danced and sang and learned about "Do Bees" and "Don't Bees." No agent went to Brooklyn to sign him to a contract as a result of his appearance on TV. But young Curtis was very impressed by his brief experience with fame.

An outgoing boy, Curtis had no trouble making friends and was popular at St. Matthew's parochial school. He was well-coordinated and good at sports. At the age of eight he was hurt by a mugger because he did not have any money, and his father ordered him to take karate lessons so he could take care of himself.

When he reached high-school age, Curtis continued his education in a private school. Although it was a sacrifice for his parents to pay the required tuition, they undoubtedly wanted him to get the best education possible. Brooklyn Preparatory School, run by Jesuits, was a very strict school, with rigid dress and behavior codes. The strictness did not bother Curtis. Through his upbringing, by both parents and grandparents, and his lessons in karate, he was used to discipline. He was a model student, and by the time he was fifteen he had also decided to be a model citizen.

Inspired by a local television program that urged private citizens to clean up their own littered neighborhoods, young Curtis Sliwa decided to start his own personal clean-up of Canarsie in 1970. With his parents' support, he began to collect trash. Every afternoon after school and on weekends he scoured the neighborhood, picking up newspapers, tin cans, bottles—whatever recyclable or reusable trash he could find. Back home he stacked the newspapers, sorted the

Curtis Sliwa, founder and leader of the Guardian Angels.

—New Jersey Newsphotos

bottles, flattened the cans and neatly arranged and stored the refuse he had collected. The Sliwas' neighbors thought all this was very nice, until the trash really began to pile up. By the time Curtis had single-handedly collected approximately five tons of trash and arranged it in his family's yard, the neighbors were saying he had gone too far. In fact, some of them were threatening legal action.

The New York *Daily News*, for which Curtis worked as a newsboy, ran an article about the situation. "Everybody was talking about the environment, but nobody was doing anything," Curtis told the reporter who covered the story. "I decided to do something." Curtis kept on collecting trash, and in 1971, when he was sixteen, he joined the New York Environmental Coalition. The *Daily News* ran another article about him at that time.

The next year, Curtis displayed another kind of citizenship. While delivering copies of the newspaper in Canarsie one day, he came upon a burning house. Instead of joining the other spectators on the sidewalk, Curtis entered the house and helped to rescue several people (three, six, or seven, depending on the source of the report). The story of the sixteen-year-old newsboy's heroism was even bigger than that of the fifteen-year-old protector of the environment. The *Daily News* gave it much attention, and so did other local newspapers. Mayor John Lindsay presented him with a Distinguished and Exceptional Service Award and Governor Nelson Rockefeller gave him a Highest Achievement Award. President Richard Nixon personally honored him as one of the nation's top eleven newsboys. Proudly, Curtis added these awards to those he had already received for his environmental efforts.

Soon thereafter he received an American Legion award as Outstanding High School Student of the Year. Curtis was certainly a likely recipient of such an award. Not only had he shown heroism and good citizenship, but he had also shown clear leadership qualities and was elected president of the student government at Brooklyn Prep in his senior year there. He says he had acceptances and scholarship offers from Brown, Princeton, and Harvard.

But Curtis Sliwa did not go on to college, nor did he finish his senior year at Brooklyn Prep. The young model citizen took his position as president of the student government so seriously that it interfered with his own academic career.

At issue were the strict rules at the school. Influenced by the student-rights movement that had begun in many colleges in the late 1960s and that was now beginning to be felt in high schools, the students at Brooklyn Prep rebelled against the dress code that required jackets and ties. Curtis Sliwa did not personally mind wearing a jacket and tie, but, he explains, "It was my duty as president to carry out what the students wanted." Besides, Curtis believed that the students should have more say. He used his position as president of the student body to demand a voice in the decisions that affected the students. "I did a lot of stupid things, and I said a lot of stupid things to the principal," he says now. The school administration would not stand for such a challenge, even if it came from a model student. Only two weeks before graduation, Curtis Sliwa was expelled from Brooklyn Prep.

Curtis's father must have felt that Curtis had thrown away the private high school diploma for which his parents had worked so hard, not to mention the college scholarship offers. Chester Sliwa insisted that Curtis finish high school—otherwise, he had better get a job and start paying rent at home.

Curtis enrolled in the public Canarsie High School. But he did not stay there long. He could not adjust to a new school so late in his senior year. He dropped out, got a job as a night manager of a Shell gas station in East New York, and started paying rent at home.

For the next few years, Curtis tried to figure out who he was and what he was going to do with the rest of his life. As a high-school dropout, he could not get a very good job. He wanted to be someone important, and he knew he was capable of handling much more responsibility. And yet he did not return to high school for his diploma. After a few months of working full time, he did not want to go back to being a student again.

In the hours when he was not working, Curtis put his extra energy into street activities, making a name for himself as a brawler. It was during this period of his life that he got the nickname "The Rock" for his fighting prowess and his ability to go for days with very little sleep. But a street reputation was not what Curtis Sliwa wanted in life. He wanted something more—something better.

Eventually, he went to work for an A&P supermarket in Canarsie and worked his way up to assistant manager. With that kind of experience, he was able to apply for other responsible jobs, and in 1978 he was hired as assistant manager at a McDonald's in the South Bronx. It was a tough neighborhood, and his job included "bouncing" loiterers and unruly customers. He proved so dedicated to his work that he was chosen to appear in training films produced by the McDonald's organization.

The commute by subway between the Bronx and his parents' home in Brooklyn was too long and too dangerous at night, so Curtis moved in with his sister, Aleta, who had an apartment in Manhattan. Canarsie was spotless compared to the South Bronx neighborhood where he worked. It was a slum area of abandoned and burned-out buildings. The people there were so hopeless about ever getting out of the cycle of poverty that long ago they had stopped worrying about litter. But Curtis Sliwa did worry, and he organized his fellow employees to clean up the area around the franchise. But he did not stop there. As assistant manager of a McDonald's he found he was in a position to influence the young people of the area. Kids who started singing "You deserve a break today" whenever they passed by were more than willing to listen to someone as important as an assistant manager at McDonald's.

Before long, Curtis had organized a group of sixty-three high-school students as his "Rock Brigade" to clean up litter in the neighborhood. Once he had his group organized, he announced a "Fordham Road Marathon Sweep," and mindful of the power of publicity, he asked his mother to type up a press release announcing the movement. The release was sent off to all the local newspapers. Some of the newspapers carried the story, and that attracted more recruits for the Rock Brigade as well as the attention of Bronx businessmen.

Curtis talked these businessmen and McDonald's into giving awards to the Brigade, and Mrs. Sliwa sent out press releases announcing the awards. Newspapers carried the story, and then Curtis announced that the Rock Brigade was expanding its territory. They were not going to clean up just the South Bronx; they were going to clean up the entire city. In December 1978 Mayor Edward Koch proclaimed the thirtieth of the month "Marathon Sweep Day," and a smiling Curtis Sliwa shook hands with the mayor and accepted Mr. Koch's faint praise: "Anything and anyone who assists in cleaning the city is doing a good deed."

Edward I. Koch does not usually make such flat, dull statements to the press. He is far better known for his controversial, colorful statements. But apparently the mayor had been caught off guard and was more than a little bewildered by Curtis Sliwa and his Rock Brigade. Who was this kid from the Bronx with his press releases and his demands for official recognition of his clean-up campaign?

After December 30, 1978, the mayor and his deputies still had no answers because Curtis Sliwa and his Rock Brigade just seemed to disappear. There were no more press releases and no more "sweeps." Just a publicity seeker, the people at City Hall decided. They forgot about Curtis Sliwa. But within two months they would hear from him again.

# The Magnificent Thirteen

Curtis Sliwa still believed that cleaning up litter on the streets was an important and needed activity, but he considered crime prevention a higher priority. It occurred to him that if he could get a bunch of teenagers to go to war against litter, then he might be able to do the same thing against crime.

He had first-hand knowledge of the amount of crime on the city's streets and subways. As night manager of a Shell station in Canarsie, he had been held up several times. And as just a private citizen walking the streets and riding the subways, he had seen muggings and purse-snatchings and all the other petty crimes that caused people to be afraid. But since going to work at a McDonald's in the South Bronx and riding the subways at night, he had come up against so much crime that he had begun to think about ways to combat it.

Curtis was not afraid for himself. He was tall and well-muscled and knew karate. Besides, he usually rode the subways with Don Chin, another McDonald's employee, when he went home from work at night. Don Chin was a big man, and no mugger would dare attack him. Curtis Sliwa looked more vulnerable, but when challenged, his knowledge of the martial arts and ability to protect himself soon drove would-be muggers away. What concerned both Chin and Sliwa were the people who were helpless. They did not like hearing the screams of women whose purses were snatched, or seeing an old derelict taunted by a young tough, or watching the frightened look on the face of a student whenever a group of strange teenagers entered the subway car.

Before long, Curtis and Don had decided to do something about crime on their subway line. They established a "decoy situation": Curtis would play the potential victim, wearing a gold watch and a three-piece suit and looking "muggable." Don, wearing Marine Corps boots and a headband, would be in another part of the car or train, connected to Curtis by a "beeper" system like doctors use. As soon as Curtis felt that he was being set up as a victim, he would signal Don, who would move in and seize the culprits or drive them away. It worked so well that Curtis started thinking in larger terms: If he and Don could be an antimugger squad of two, just imagine what several people could do.

They couldn't be just any group of people, of course. They would have to know how to defend themselves. They would have to be calm, mature people who would not get scared or excited. They would have to have sense enough to remember that their purpose was to turn the captured mugger into the transit police and not to beat him up. They would have to be "from the community" so that they would not frighten or put off the very people they were trying to protect. They would have to be loyal to each other and dedicated to a common cause. What Curtis Sliwa needed, actually, was a gang— but a gang committed to preventing crime, not causing it.

After he was so successful in organizing the Rock Brigade, Curtis Sliwa thought and talked much about his idea of an anticrime gang. Don Chin thought he was crazy and took to calling Curtis's imaginary anticrime gang the "Kamikaze Kids." But Curtis was so certain his idea was worthwhile that he did not need his friend's approval. He went on with his plans without the help of Don Chin.

Curtis Sliwa put considerable thought into the planning of his anticrime gang. He realized that he needed a carefully chosen name, a recognizable uniform or colors, a strong organization, and strict rules. After considering and rejecting several names, he went on to the question of colors. An admirer of the Green Berets, an elite combat troop that served in Vietnam, he chose red berets as part of the uniform for the group. Also, as he put it, the red berets "stand out like lollipops" in a crowd. He also decided on white T-shirts with red writing, because the young people he would recruit would not have the money to buy special jackets.

As the symbol for the group, he chose an all-seeing eye. His group's purpose would be to see, and thus prevent, potential crimes. Also, an eye, all by itself, has little racial or sexual distinction. "I chose it because you can't see if it's black or white, male or female," Curtis explained.

The group would be tightly organized. Curtis would be the leader, of course, and below him would be patrol captains. Everyone would have to follow the rules he laid down. They would not carry weapons. If they saw a crime in progress, they would alert the transit police, or they would make a citizen's arrest if they could do it safely. An ordinary citizen may arrest someone whom he sees committing a crime, providing that the person arrested is immediately turned over to the police or other agency of the law. But the group's main purpose would be to deter crime. Curtis hoped that their very presence on the subways would cause muggers to think twice before snatching a woman's purse or rolling a drunk.

Curtis Sliwa did not find many young people for his group. Besides his own exacting standards, there was the fact that many were not attracted to the idea of an anticrime patrol. They would have to volunteer their time, even pay the subway fare in order to patrol the trains. Many thought the patrol sounded too much like a kind of auxiliary police force, and the police were not very popular in the South Bronx. In the end, only twelve youths were both willing to join Sliwa and able to meet his requirements. They included an eighteen-year-old black youth named Tony who had a black belt in karate and an eighteen-year-old Puerto Rican youth named Arnaldo who wanted to be an FBI agent. Another eighteen-year-old Puerto Rican youth who had joined the group had been president of his high school's computer-science club and had been accepted at the prestigious Massachusetts Institute of Technology. Every one of them was mature and able to take care of himself. Sliwa decided to call the group the "Magnificent Thirteen."

They began patrolling in February 1979, and it was no accident that Curtis chose the thirteenth day of the month to launch the patrols. He also asked his mother to send out press releases announcing the formation of the group and its purpose. "We are prepared to sacrifice our lives if necessary," read the release, which Curtis wrote. It continued, "In the same spirit that our nation's forefathers resisted the tyranny of the Crown, so shall we resist the tyranny of fear that rules our subways."

Patrols from eight p.m. to four a.m. began on the so-called "Muggers' Express," the No. 4 IRT (Interboro Rapid Transit) line from Woodlawn Avenue in the Bronx down the length of Manhattan Island to Atlantic Avenue in Brooklyn. The very first night, according to their own reports, one three-man patrol stopped a mugging at 167th Street and River Avenue in the Bronx. While restraining the mugger, they asked the train's conductor to signal ahead to the next station where a transit patrolman was on duty. There, they handed the mugger over to the police.

A week later, a twenty-year-old white youth named Karl Smucker was assaulted while on routine patrol in a station. Although the

A Guardian Angel stands watch in a New York City subway.     —*Detroit News*

others in his patrol quickly grabbed the culprit, Smucker's arm was broken in two places.

In March, Curtis Sliwa and another member of the Magnificent Thirteen rescued a subway clerk who had fallen onto the tracks at Manhattan's Union Square station, right in the path of an oncoming express train.

Each of these incidents was reported in press releases prepared by Curtis and his mother, and within a month just about everyone who read the newspapers had heard of the Magnificent Thirteen. Curtis obliged the newspaper reporters with quotes such as, "Volunteer patrols seemed the only way to show that the public's had enough" and "Our main weapon is our presence. We don't want to fight anyone if we can help it, but just being around puts the muggers off."

After the group started getting publicity, so many people came to see Curtis Sliwa at work that the company transferred him to another franchise. Many youths wanted to join the Magnificent Thirteen. Curtis chose new members carefully and turned down more than he accepted. They had to have a job or be going to school. They had to have some training in the martial arts, and they had to show that they would not react to verbal abuse, especially racial name-calling. They could not put on the red beret if they were doing so because they had a grudge—perhaps because some friend or family member had been mugged. Still, by late April the group numbered forty-eight, including a sizable number of Chinese youths who had read about the Magnificent Thirteen in Chinatown newspapers. Admitting the Chinese required Curtis Sliwa to prove himself, in a way. He had to meet with the Gray Shadows, the most powerful gang in Chinatown, and assure the gang that his group was not interested in Chinatown "turf." By early May 1979, the Magnificent Thirteen had received national exposure in *Time* magazine. Soon, they had a new name—the "Guardian Angels." Curtis Sliwa's religious schooling made it a likely choice.

Not all the publicity the group received was favorable. The Transit Authority Police and the New York City Police, as well as Mayor Koch, were very much against them and their activities. They called the Guardian Angels a vigilante group and said they would do more harm than good. It is true that some vigilante groups do more harm than good by arming themselves and trying to take the law into their own hands. In this way they bypass an individual's constitutional right to trial by jury. Often vigilantes wind up getting hurt, or hurting innocent people, or punishing criminals more harshly than the law decrees. But it really was incorrect to label the Angels a vigilante group, for they were not armed and were intent only on making citizens' arrests, if necessary. Their main purpose was to act as watchdogs. But the authorities remained unconvinced, and official recognition of the Guardian Angels was denied until a much later date.

A member of the Guardian Angels leads fellow members in a martial-arts class in a New York City park.      *—Wide World Photos, Inc.*

# The Guardian Angels

Whether or not city officials recognized the Guardian Angels, the press and the public did. Local newspapers and television stations frequently reported on their activities, and the average subway rider had nothing but praise for the kids who were volunteering their time to help protect them. The very presence of the red berets on the subways at night was warmly reassuring.

Curtis Sliwa decided to put pressure on the city officials. In September 1979 he organized a three-day hunger strike at City Hall to protest Mayor Koch's refusal to credit the Guardian Angels with rescuing a Transit Authority patrolman. On July 16, according to the Angels, Patrolman Robert Miller was being beaten with his own nightstick by three thugs at the Bowling Green IRT station in Manhattan. The Angels stepped in and saved his life. The patrolman insisted that at no time had the incident gotten out of control, although he was glad to see the Angel patrol come to his aid.

Although the mayor and other city officials did not like to be pressured in this way, they were forced to soften their stand. The

23

deputy police commissioner stated publicly that the Angels had broken up 104 potential crimes. And Chief James Meehan of the Transit Authority Police told a reporter for *The New York Times,* "We think they act as a deterrent." Representatives from the New York City Police, the Transit Authority Police, and the mayor's office began meeting with Curtis Sliwa in October 1979 to work out some way in which the Angels and the regular law-enforcement agencies could cooperate.

The officials were worried that any youth could put on a white T-shirt and red beret and use the uniform to commit crimes against unsuspecting subway riders. So they suggested that the Angels be given official identification cards. They also suggested that the Angels receive training in self-defense from the regular police. But Curtis Sliwa rejected this plan. He wanted to keep the Angels free from government interference. His Angels came from neighborhoods where the police were viewed as the enemy. If the Guardian Angels were nothing more than an auxiliary police force, they would lose the respect of their friends, and they wouldn't want to be Angels any longer.

However, by the middle of January 1980, Curtis Sliwa had changed his mind. In the eleven months since he had started his subway patrol, the group had grown from 13 members to some 700, including a small percentage of young women. He had quit his job at McDonald's and was living on his savings, plus loans from friends and relatives, in order to spend all his time running the organization. He now had his own apartment on University Avenue in the Bronx. From there, and from a telephone booth at the Columbus Circle subway station in Manhattan, he directed as many as 100 patrols every night. He had memorized almost every station location and train schedule on the 230-mile system, and tracked the progress of all patrols nightly. But Curtis was just one individual, and he realized that he could not keep tabs on all 700 Angels, not to mention anyone who might pretend to be one. So he agreed to some form of government monitoring. But he would not give control of the Angels to any government authority. "We will remain independent," he declared. "City officials should have the right to know where we are, when we are patrolling, and who we are. They do not have the right to tell us when and where to do it."

But though both sides agreed in principle that there should be some sort of formal relationship between the Angels and regular law-enforcement agencies, the details were hard to work out. The problem was, where do self-appointed defenders of the law fit into law enforcement? The police unions wanted to be sure that the Guardian Angels would not replace police officers or affect the hiring of police. Curtis Sliwa wanted the Angels to be able to ride the subways free. Negotiations went on for months, but by the fall there was still no agreement.

Guardian Angels conferring while on street patrol in New York City.

*—Detroit News*

Meanwhile, the Guardian Angels continued their patrols and got high praise from subway riders and the media. Jimmy Breslin, a columnist for the New York *Daily News,* suggested that the police felt their manhood was threatened by the young crusaders. Barry Farber, a local radio personality, hosted a fund-raising drive that brought in $14,000 for the Angels.

A few public officials were also firmly on the side of the Angels. In September 1980 at a dinner honoring Curtis Sliwa which was sponsored by the local East-Side Manhattan newspaper *Our Town,* the lieutenant governor of New York State, Mario Cuomo, announced: "These are not vigilantes. They have decided, without compensation and at great risk to themselves, to perform a major public service. They are the best society has to offer. We should be encouraging their kind of strength and their kind of courage." Cuomo also addressed openly the race and class conflict that was woven into the controversy over the Angels: "If these were the sons and daughters of doctors from Great Neck or Jamaica Estates, would people be calling them vigilantes? Everyone would be giving them medals."

Many of the supporters of the Guardian Angels charged that racism and classism were at the root of the objections of those who were against them. The Angels were primarily minority youth, and it was the idea of a large, organized group of blacks and Hispanics that really worried their critics. Earl Caldwell, another columnist for the *Daily News*, pointed out that the chief critics of the Angels were people who did not have to ride the subways or walk the streets of unsafe neighborhoods at night.

But Mayor Koch, for one, insisted that racism was not at the root of his objections. He thought the Angels were just out for publicity. "Good Samaritans don't ask for rewards," he said. One of the Angels, Koch added, had already sold his life story to television, and the mayor did not feel like helping to sell a television show.

That one Angel was Curtis Sliwa. Highgate Pictures, Inc., a subsidiary of the Learning Corporation of America, wanted to make a TV movie about him and the Guardian Angels. Curtis Sliwa had signed a contract and accepted an advance payment. Later, he turned around and spent most of it to sue Highgate Pictures, Inc. The movie, which was aired in April 1981, depicted its fictional hero as starting his subway patrol after he was threatened by gangs and his father was mugged. Curtis Sliwa strongly believed that revenge should not be a reason for starting an anticrime patrol. As of this writing, the court suit has not been resolved, and Curtis Sliwa has turned down all other offers to do movies about his life.

Although Curtis insisted that he was not just seeking publicity, he was getting a lot of it. In a single, typical week that fall of 1980 he was interviewed by Japanese, Norwegian, and Spanish newspapers, not to mention national wire service reporters and local television newsmen. He appeared at fund-raising events and traveled with his lawyer to Washington, D.C., to try to get the Guardian Angels declared a tax-exempt organization. (In February 1981 the Alliance of Guardian Angels, Inc. became a nonprofit, tax-exempt corporation.)

Perhaps Curtis Sliwa was so busy with other things that he could not pay undivided attention to his young members. Or perhaps individual transit patrolmen just got tired of all the favorable publicity the Angels were getting and decided to stick a pin in the Guardian Angels' balloon. Whatever the reasons, in early October 1980 there began a series of scattered confrontations between New York City Transit Authority Police and the Angels.

On October 5 a seventeen-year-old Angel named Nelson Toga was accused by two transit patrolmen of smoking in the BMT (Brooklyn and Manhattan Transit) Pacific Street station. According to the patrolmen, Toga assaulted them. But after a woman came forward to testify that Toga had been roughed up by two transit patrolmen as he was escorting her through a Brooklyn subway station late at night, the charges against Toga were dropped.

On October 19 according to Curtis Sliwa, three men stopped him at 11:45 p.m. at the Fordham Road IRT station in the Bronx. They said they were transit police (one of them showed him a gold shield), and they told him that a Guardian Angel had been seriously hurt on patrol. They offered to take him to the hospital where the Angel had been admitted, and Sliwa went with them. But, he reported, when they drove right past the hospital he began to suspect that something was wrong. The three men took him all the way to Jones Beach on Long Island, an hour's ride. Before they released him they warned him that the Angels should stop patrolling because they were taking jobs away from transit officers.

Bronx District Attorney Mario Merola was a supporter of the Guardian Angels, but the investigation he ordered did not produce the three men. William McKechnie, president of the Transit Authority's Patrolmen's Benevolent Association, did not believe Sliwa's story and said: "Curtis Sliwa knows by heart the phone numbers of every newspaper, radio and television station, reporter and editor in the city. It seems incredible that he should not remember the license plate of the car or the badge numbers of the officers."

Leaving headquarters, the Guardian Angels start a night patrol.   —*Detroit News*

In mid-January 1981 Police Commissioner Robert McGuire announced another plan to register and train the Guardian Angels, and for a month there were no further clashes between the Angels and the transit police. But the uneasy peace was soon broken. On February 13, 1981, exactly two years after the original Magnificent Thirteen began their patrols, ten members of the Guardian Angels were arrested by transit police after a melee on an IND (Independent) subway train in Brooklyn.

The transit police charged that the Angels had gotten into a fight with passengers who objected to the way the Angels were treating a drunk, and that the police had simply moved in to restore order. Curtis Sliwa, who was not present at the scene, insisted that the disturbance began after Angels on patrol stumbled into and unintentionally disrupted a police decoy operation. Although at first this charge was denied, later the transit police admitted that there were indeed three plainclothes officers in the car. Charges against the Angels were later dropped. The incident proved how important it was for the Angels and the New York City Transit Police to have greater communication. There was no need for undercover police and Angels to be operating in the same car when crimes were being committed on other subway cars all over the city.

On February 15, 1981, a seventeen-year-old youth who said he was a Guardian Angel and who was wearing a red beret, was arrested while trying to break into an unattended token booth at Manhattan's Fulton Street station. As it turned out, the youth was not a Guardian Angel. This incident pointed up the importance of the Angels' carrying some sort of official identification.

But still Curtis Sliwa and the officials of New York City could not come to an agreement on the details of a plan of cooperation. As they continued to negotiate through the winter and into the spring of 1981 public pressure increased, and it was mostly on the side of the Angels. Even people who were very worried about the potential problems that might come from official recognition of the Angels were urging some kind of agreement. As an editorial in *The New York Times* put it, "Guiding this spontaneous and admittedly risky movement to constructive service is simply another challenge to New York. It certainly beats the alternative—leaving restless but organized youth to make trouble. . . So we salute the red berets— warily."

Finally, Curtis Sliwa decided to take action. One night in late May he led 450 Guardian Angels in an all-night vigil at Gracie Mansion, the official residence of Mayor Koch. They stood in silence, each holding a candle. The majority of them were black and Hispanic. The mayor had been confronted with demonstrations by minority people in the past, but they had been very loud, angry demonstrations. He had walked out on them, saying he would not deal with angry mobs. Curtis Sliwa later explained to *Daily News* columnist Jimmy Breslin that such incidents had given him an idea about how to get to the mayor. He would confront him with 450 blacks and Hispanics, "but not with everybody screaming in some auditorium where he could walk out. I was going to make Koch go to sleep at night with four hundred and fifty blacks and Hispanics right under his bedroom window. When his car drove past us into his driveway that night, he was slumped down. We could see his head, but not his mouth."

Whether or not the silent vigil at Gracie Mansion had anything to do with it, on May 29, 1981, the Office of the Mayor announced the signing of a "memorandum of understanding" among the Guardian Angels, the Police Department, and the Transit Authority Police that would allow all parties to "work together cooperatively." Among other things, it provided for registration of Angels with the Police Department, which would issue red and white identification cards to be worn while on duty.

The agreement also provided that members of the Guardian Angels would be given police records checks to make sure that no one who had been convicted of a serious crime would remain an Angel or try to become one. The New York City Police Department ran checks on approximately 550 Guardian Angels over the next few months and found that only 26 had any criminal records at all. Of these, only 6 Angels had records for serious offenses. Curtis Sliwa dismissed all 6 from the Guardian Angels.

Official acceptance of the Guardian Angels was grudging. According to Curtis Sliwa, Mayor Koch said to him, "You're like chicken soup. When a person has a cold it can't hurt, it can only help." But grudging or not, the acceptance was official. It had been a long fight, but Curtis and his Angels had won.

A volunteer safety patrol of Guardian Angels in "Mugger's Alley" in New York City.                                                    *—Wide World Photos, Inc.*

# The Angels Spread Their Wings

Long before New York City gave official recognition to the Guardian Angels, Curtis Sliwa had started expanding his organization to other cities. It was not just his own ambition that was behind this expansion. Young people in nearby areas were excited by the idea of the Guardian Angels and wanted to form their own anticrime patrols. By June 1980, Hoboken, New Jersey, just across the Hudson River from Manhattan by PATH subway, had a Guardian Angels chapter. Not long after that, Newark, New Jersey, had a chapter as well.

As the New York City Guardian Angels received more and more publicity on national television and in the national press, Curtis Sliwa began to get inquiries from young people and community groups in cities as far away as New Orleans, Chicago, and San Francisco. Excited by the idea of a national organization, in 1980 Sliwa began traveling to places like Hartford, Connecticut, and Philadelphia, Pennsylvania, to organize new chapters of the Guardian Angels. But he was hampered by two major problems.

The first was money. It cost money to go around the country

organizing new chapters. He did a lot of hitchhiking, and he relied greatly on the hospitality of supporters once he got to other cities. Although the Guardian Angels received private contributions, the amount was not enough to finance a national campaign. One reason why Sliwa applied for tax-exempt status for his organization was so people and businesses who gave money to the Guardian Angels could deduct the sums from their income-tax payments.

The second problem was that in spite of the growth of the Guardian Angels it was still very much a one-man operation. Curtis Sliwa was the founder, director, and chief spokesman. He directed the patrols, granted interviews with the media, wrote the press releases (with help from his mother, who by now was working full-time as the Angels' unpaid secretary), met and negotiated with city officials, and personally presided over the organization of new chapters of the Guardian Angels. Even working eighteen hours a day, seven days a week, he could barely keep up with his present responsibilities. He could not take on any more. He needed a second-in-command whom he could trust to speak for him and act in his behalf, someone with political savvy, someone who was as attractive and articulate as he was. He found that person in Lisa Evers.

Lisa, a year older than Curtis, grew up in Chicago. The oldest of six children of a machinery salesman and a nurse in a methadone clinic, she attended college on a scholarship and graduated with a degree in economics. After her mother died in 1978, Lisa went east to Manhattan, where she got a cheap apartment on the slum-ridden Lower East Side and worked as a waitress because it was the only work she could find. At college she had taken a number of art courses, and in New York she made friends with artists and soon became director of an art studio. She also became a regular at the fashionable disco Studio 54. But she continued to live in the dangerous Lower East Side neighborhood. Instead of moving to a safer area, she took up karate. She also did not allow her association with the "beautiful people" to make her blind to the problems of the less fortunate people. Her parents had taught her to "challenge yourself and help other people," so anyone who knew her well was not surprised when, in the summer of 1980, Lisa Evers joined the Guardian Angels.

Lisa Evers explains responsibilities to a Detroit youngster. *—Detroit News*

Lisa was not the first female to join the group. Despite newspaper descriptions of the Guardian Angels as a group of young men, there were a few young women by the time she joined. But Lisa Evers stood out among them. She had a black belt in karate, for one thing, and when Curtis Sliwa was her opponent at the required martial-arts training sessions, he found himself on the floor a lot. She was also completely unafraid of arguing with him. While most new recruits treated Curtis Sliwa like some sort of god, Lisa Evers was not in the least awed by the "leader." In fact, she thought he acted like a dictator and told him so. He told *her* that it was his organization and that he didn't care what she liked. Curtis recalls, "You couldn't find two people in the world who disliked each other more than we did."

Although she did not think much of Curtis Sliwa, Lisa Evers did believe in the goals of his organization, and she stuck it out. Gradually, as the political struggle between Sliwa and the New York City officials continued, and as the Angels received more and more publicity, Lisa began to understand the pressures that Curtis was under. She stopped thinking of him as a dictator. For his part, Curtis came to respect Lisa's commitment to the Angels and to admire her ability to speak about it. When Curtis realized he was going to have to share some of his authority if he was going to be able to do everything he wanted to do, he chose Lisa Evers to be his second-in-command. In March 1981 Lisa was named National Director of the Guardian Angels.

Of course there was some grumbling in the Angels ranks about having a woman as Sliwa's chief lieutenant, but this grumbling was not done in public or in Curtis Sliwa's hearing. The official policy of the Guardian Angels was that females were welcome in the organization, and if they were welcome, then of course they could be at the top. Curtis Sliwa set the official policy, and he tolerated no opposition. He also was very ready to admit that the Guardian Angels organization was not a democracy.

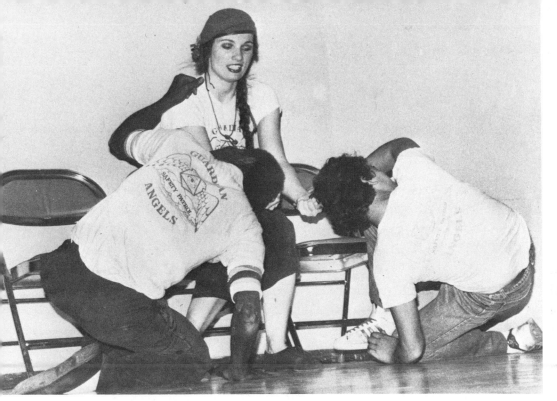

Lisa Evers demonstrates self-defense techniques at a New York City seminar.
—*N.Y. Daily News Photo*

For his part, he took great pains to be a proper role model for his young followers, never demanding of them anything he was not willing to do himself. Although he was attracted to Lisa and she to him, they both realized that the organization could be badly affected if they were to start dating and then break up. So they confined their talk to the business of the Guardian Angels.

With Lisa Evers as his second-in-command, Curtis Sliwa could now "spread the wings" of the Angels wide. Like many other Americans, he and the Angels were concerned and frustrated over the rash of child killings in Atlanta, Georgia. The Angels had started wearing green ribbons on their T-shirts or berets as an expression of solidarity with the victims' families. But they wanted to do more—they wanted to go to Atlanta and organize street patrols. One of Lisa Evers' first assignments as National Director of the Guardian Angels was to go to Atlanta with eleven other New York Angels in March 1981 and oversee the establishment of such patrols. Atlanta officials insisted that they did not need outside groups to patrol the city. Besides, said the officials, Atlanta did not have subways. But Lisa was an articulate spokesperson for the Angels' point of view. Through the media, Lisa Evers was introduced to the nation, and she helped promote the image of the Guardian Angels as a serious, public-spirited group, and not just a bunch of vigilantes. But it had been a difficult assignment for Lisa, and the experience caused her to reflect on Curtis's problems. She recalls, "I finally understood, when I was on the hot seat, how intense the pressures were that *he* was under."

Returning to New York, Lisa took on the day-to-day operation of the Guardian Angels there while Curtis began an extended period of organizing in other cities.

In New Jersey, he oversaw the establishment of Guardian Angels chapters in Jersey City and Trenton, in Paterson, Camden, and Perth Amboy. He began discussions with New Brunswick officials and community leaders about a chapter there. By June there were about 150 Guardian Angels in the state. The New Jersey Guardian Angels claimed to have made twenty-two citizens' arrests by June 1981.

Only in Trenton did the Angels find full and willing cooperation from city officials, the police, and community groups. "It happened the way it's supposed to happen," said Curtis Sliwa. Trenton was also the only city in New Jersey to welcome the aid of the new Metro Task Force composed of state police to fight crime.

But for every city that welcomed him and the Guardian Angels, Curtis Sliwa found four that did not, or that greeted them with mixed feelings. He was in Boston in late May and early June and received a frosty reception to his plan to train Boston-area Angels to patrol Boston Commons, nicknamed the "Combat Zone," and the business and theater districts.

From Boston he hitchhiked to Chicago, where he envisioned Guardian Angels patrolling the infamous "Loop" and downtown Chicago, as well as the subway and elevated train systems and the

Curtis Sliwa and other Guardian Angels in Boston tell of plans to set up a chapter there. —*Wide World Photos, Inc.*

most crime-ridden housing projects. Chicago's Mayor Jane Byrne had recently launched an anticrime drive by taking an apartment in the notorious Cabrini-Green Housing Project. Curtis Sliwa announced that the Guardian Angels would establish their headquarters in an apartment in the same project.

Mayor Byrne and other city officials did not welcome Curtis Sliwa. Mayor Byrne said she did not encourage people to "come and do the work of the police department." Police Superintendent Richard Brzeczek called the Angels a "foreign vigilante group." Sighed Curtis Sliwa, "It's the same old scenario."

But Curtis knew better than to criticize city officials. That would only hurt his cause. In fact, he took great pains to challenge the opinion held by many people that "City Hall" or "the politicians" were responsible for crime anywhere.

"I blame the people for crime," he told reporters at a press conference in Chicago. "It used to be you wouldn't rip off a store because everyone would know. . . You would be ill-thought of in the community. But today, it's an honor for a kid to have a jail record. They brag about it.

"Suppose a kid is playing his radio too loud. The police come, tell him to shut it off or they'll haul him in. You know what the kid does? He turns it down, and when the cop walks away. . . But if the people in the neighborhood come over and surround him like you're all surrounding me now, well, what do you think's going to happen?"

As Curtis was called upon again and again to defend his organization, he developed and refined his own ideas about its goals and its functions. By the spring of 1981, he had decided that Angels didn't just need training in discipline, the martial arts, and citizen's-arrest law. They also needed training in CPR (cardiopulmonary resuscitation) because Angels patrols came upon many more victims of heart attack and diabetic coma than crimes in progress, and he felt that they ought to be able to help out.

Further, he realized he would not be able to control a national organization as loosely organized as the original group. So, the first fifty members of any new Angels chapter must have no police record at all and must be recommended for membership by community leaders. Thereafter, the chapter could set its own membership rules, but no one guilty of a serious crime could be a member.

But nothing he could say seemed to soften the attitude of Chicago public officials. As in New York and elsewhere, it was the press and the public that came to the defense of Sliwa and the Angels. Curtis had to leave Chicago in the midst of the controversy, for he was due in New Orleans, Louisiana, to start an Angels chapter there.

New Orleans is too hot in mid-June to be called a vacation spot, but to Curtis, being in New Orleans was like being on vacation from the criticism and suspicion he had found in Chicago. New Orleans welcomed him. Orleans Parish Sheriff Charles Foti guided him through some of the city's high-crime areas. City Councilman Mike Early introduced him to the rest of the council's members saying, "I think the Angels are a healthy antidote to the Me Generation and their non-involvement." The New Orleans press helped, too, by reporting that the three Guardian Angels chapters in Los Angeles had been granted approval by the Los Angeles Police Department.

Although his reception in New Orleans had been one of the best he had received, he still took pains to assure the city's police that the Angels had no desire to take any power from them. The Angels would not go to neighborhood disturbances, nor arrest prostitutes. An individual could "roll a wheelbarrow full of cocaine" past an Angel's nose and he would do nothing about it. When Curtis left New Orleans, promising to return later in the year to preside over graduation ceremonies for the new Angels chapter there, he felt more certain than ever that what he was doing was right. And it is somehow fitting that in the first few months of their existence, the New Orleans Angels proved their value by arresting a robber with a record of fifty-seven previous arrests and a pickpocket who turned out to be a murder suspect wanted by the police.

Curtis Sliwa's hopeful feeling continued as, back in New York, he served as best man at the first Guardian Angels wedding. On a Saturday afternoon in late June, twenty-four-year-old Rocky Pratt of the Bronx and eighteen-year-old Juanita Ortiz of Brooklyn took marriage vows in a Brooklyn church. Then they and a wedding party of some twenty-five, including a number of other Angels, boarded the subway for a reception at Fifth Avenue and 59th Street. The couple had met while on patrol eighteen months before, and while the bride chose to wear a traditional wedding veil that day, the groom sported his elaborately decorated red beret. Adorned with silver stars and studs, it was Rocky Pratt's way of expressing his individuality.

Indeed, the variety of beret decorations on Fifth Avenue that day rivaled those on the hats in the traditional Easter Parade. Although Curtis Sliwa insisted on absolute discipline in the Angels organization, he also realized that his young troops needed some way to separate themselves from one another, so he allowed them to decorate their berets in any way they chose. The berets were masterpieces of creativity and artistic effort. Studded, beaded, adorned with medals and even raccoon tails, they were completely personal statements on the part of the 700 young people who proudly patrolled the New York City subways and parks.

Guardian Angels march through downtown New Orleans carrying a symbolic coffin.
                                                                    *—Laura Elliott*

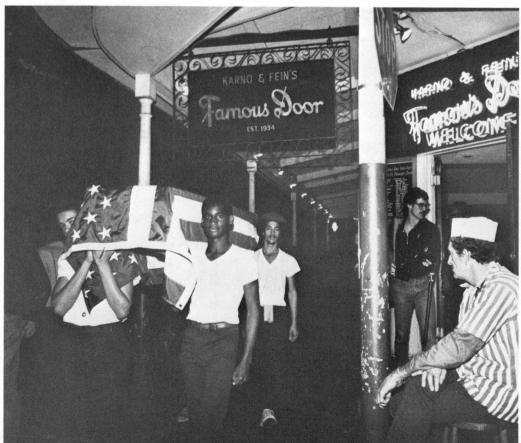

# Growing Pains and Pleasures

In early July 1981 Curtis Sliwa was in San Francisco, organizing a Guardian Angels chapter there. Mayor Dianne Feinstein gave him a pleasant but cautious reception. But before he could accomplish much in California, Curtis was called back to New York for the funeral of a former Guardian Angel who had been killed.

Malcolm Brown, nineteen, from Brooklyn, had been a Guardian Angel patrol leader until February. He had quit the Angels because his girlfriend had complained that the subway patrols were too dangerous. But though he quit the Angels, Malcolm Brown could not stop being a concerned citizen. When he saw three men trying to rob two women, he stepped in and was shot to death. "There were maybe thirty or forty people there, but no one would jump in or get involved," said Curtis. "That's why he's dead." Some 200 Guardian Angels from six cities held a memorial funeral procession for Malcolm Brown, carrying a flag-draped, empty coffin through the streets of Brooklyn as a testimony to their fallen comrade.

The coffin was a very effective symbol of the victims of crime.

Curtis began to hold mock funeral processions in the cities where new Guardian Angels chapters were being organized. In late October there was one in Chicago, and in late November New Orleans was treated to a similar procession.

Guardian Angels march against violence in Los Angeles. Their aim is to stop violence by persuading the public to get involved.    *—Wide World Photos, Inc.*

On July 9, 1981, after the funeral of Malcolm Brown, Curtis went to Washington, D.C., to testify as the main witness before a Senate Judiciary juvenile crime subcommittee. He stated that as far as he was concerned the only way to stop the rising crime rate was "at the community level by the participation of the citizens." While in the nation's capital, he was approached by community leaders about starting an Angels chapter there, and in early August he returned for preliminary talks with police officials. It was then that he was kidnapped a second time.

According to Curtis, he found himself in the capital very late one night; in fact, it was after midnight. He did not realize that the Washington, D.C., subways stopped running after a certain hour, and he did not have the cab fare for the trip back to where he was staying, so he decided to walk. As he neared the Lincoln Memorial, four men approached him, said they were police officers, and announced that they were going to arrest him. They held him for several hours, poked him with a cattle prod, beat him up, and threw him into the Potomac River.

Although there was no question that Curtis had been beaten and bruised, the National Park Service Police, who investigated the case, were unable to find the kidnappers, or any proof that Sliwa's abductors had been police officers.

Two nights later, with his arm in a sling and his neck in a brace, Curtis was in Baltimore, organizing an Angels chapter there. Two weeks after that, he and Lisa Evers were in Sacramento, California. During a live interview at the studios of KGNR radio, Curtis collapsed in mid-sentence and was rushed to a nearby hospital. Doctors told the press that he had fainted from nervous exhaustion and that he'd had flashbacks about the beating in Washington, D.C., two weeks before.

More and more, Curtis Sliwa was coming to rely on Lisa Evers, and the way she was able to take over for him when he collapsed was one reason why. She shared his commitment to the Guardian Angels and understood, better than anyone else it seemed, the pressures he was under. "She's like my twin," Curtis has said of Lisa. As they worked closely together, they felt a strong attraction to one another. But because they worried about the effect on the organization, it was months before they started dating. By the fall of 1981, they were sure that they shared a love that would last, and on Christmas Eve they were married. Their wedding cake was topped by two miniature red-bereted Angels.

They spent their honeymoon in St. Louis, where they had arranged for the Guardian Angels to establish their headquarters in the Vaughn public housing project, the site of twenty-six murders in 1981.

Less than a week later, the first active Guardian Angel was killed in the line of duty. On the night of December 30, 1981, Frank Melvin, age twenty-seven, was shot and killed by a Newark, New Jersey, policeman at a housing project for senior citizens. The policeman and his partner, who were responding to a report of a break-in, said that it was a case of mistaken identity.

One of the officers was on the street, the other on a nearby rooftop. The patrolman on the rooftop said he saw a man running toward his partner in a threatening way and so he shot the man, who turned out to be Frank Melvin. But Curtis Sliwa charged that Melvin had been shot deliberately and "in cold blood." Melvin had blown his whistle and then opened his jacket to display his Guardian Angels T-shirt as he ran toward the officer on the street, according to the Angels who had been on patrol with him.

During the formal investigation into the shooting by Newark and county officials, the county coroner stated that the angle of the bullet as it entered Frank Melvin's body indicated that the fatal shot had come not from a rooftop but from street level. But the two patrolmen involved stuck to their story. A second coroner examined Frank Melvin's body and his findings supported the police version of what happened. He called the first coroner's decision "hasty" and inaccurate. But Curtis Sliwa would not be deterred from his idea that the authorities were trying to hide the real facts. He called for a march by Guardian Angels to the New Jersey state capital at Trenton to demand a state investigation. He and Lisa gave round-the-clock interviews pressing their cause, but officials at Trenton refused to open the state inquiry the Angels wanted. So Curtis called for a march to Washington, D.C.

Guardian Angels attend the funeral of Frank Melvin in Newark, New Jersey.
*—New Jersey Newsphotos*

Curtis and sixty-three other Angels started out for the nation's capital, but below-zero temperatures took their toll along the 127-mile route. Although Lisa brought a van from Manhattan with warm clothes, food, and medicine, five Angels had to be hospitalized for frostbite along the way. Only about half the original number made it to Washington. Assistant Attorney General William Bradford Reynolds met with the group, but he would not agree to open a federal investigation. In early February 1982 an Essex County grand jury found no grounds for indicting the two Newark police officers who had been involved in the shooting of Frank Melvin.

Still, Curtis believed that he and the Angels had made their point. No one could harm a Guardian Angel without the Angels' raising a sizeable protest about it. The killing of Frank Melvin would not signal, as Lisa put it, "open season on Angels."

The Sliwas returned to New York to set up a trust fund for Frank Melvin's wife and three children. By now they were living in Lisa's apartment on Manhattan's Lower East Side, primarily because it was close to the Judson Memorial Church in Greenwich Village. The church had offered the Guardian Angels the use of its basement and gym rent-free. It was the first official headquarters for the Angels that was not Curtis Sliwa's apartment.

Then Curtis and Lisa set out together on a five-day swing to Dallas, St. Louis, and Miami to visit new Angels chapters in various stages of organization. This was unusual, because as a rule Lisa "holds the fort" in New York while Curtis travels. He states, and she agrees, that their respective duties are of equal importance. He also says that he views his wife as his equal in every way. But he did insist that Lisa take his last name when they married. "When people think of the Guardian Angels, they think of Curtis Sliwa," he explained. "That's the way it is."

Guardian Angels on protest march to Trenton, New Jersey.

—*New Jersey Newsphotos*

# Hosts of Angels?

With Lisa at the command post in New York City and overseeing day-to-day operations there, Curtis began crisscrossing the nation, expanding the network of Guardian Angels chapters. Houston, Miami, suburbs of Philadelphia and Los Angeles, Cleveland, and towns in Louisiana and New Jersey needed groups like the Guardian Angels. Curtis Sliwa aimed to satisfy that need.

But even now that he was freer to travel, he was only one man, and so he was willing to help set up new chapters, but he knew he could not control them. In fact, he did not wish to control them. He wanted them to be free to develop according to the needs of their individual communities. He had certain basic requirements. Once these requirements had been met, new chapters could make their own decisions about what relationship they had with local law-enforcement agencies, where and when they would patrol, how they would raise funds, and even (beyond the required red beret and Guardian Angels T-shirt) what they would wear.

The basic requirement for setting up a new Guardian Angels

chapter is a clearly-expressed need on the part of established community groups. When, in the early summer of 1981, Louisianans outside New Orleans began asking for Guardian Angels chapters, Sliwa decided that a chapter should be started in any town from which he had received at least ten requests.

Once the process of setting up a new chapter has begun, Sliwa insists on certain requirements for membership. Potential members must have no police record, must have a job or be going to school, and must have at least three character references. But according to Lisa Sliwa, "The main screening element is time. They have to go through a three-month training program where they have to get along with people from all different neighborhoods, occupations, backgrounds. If they're not dedicated, if they have a personality problem or some other problem that is not evident from the references and the records checks, we're going to find out about it when they're on their 200th push-up and ready to break."

In addition to push-ups, Guardian Angels recruits go through martial-arts training and training in emergency medical procedures. They also learn the details of the citizen's-arrest laws in their particular states. This law differs from state to state. Handcuffs may be used when making citizens' arrests in New Jersey, so some Guardian Angels in that state carry them. Handcuffs are not legal in New York State, and if a Guardian Angels patrol leader in New York finds an Angel carrying handcuffs, the leader immediately suspends the offender. It is another basic requirement for all Guardian Angels chapters that patrol leaders frisk the members of their patrols to make sure the members are not carrying weapons or other illegal items like drugs. Finally, all Guardian Angels are required to wear the red beret and white T-shirt emblazoned with the Angels logo while on patrol.

Although Curtis Sliwa insists on thorough training of new recruits, there is evidence that this training is not always as complete as it

Guardian Angels hold a man who did not pay his subway fare.

*—N.Y. Daily News Photo*

should be. In Chicago, a reporter for the *Sun-Times* named Michael Cordts went undercover and became a Guardian Angel recruit in order to report on the training. He reported that the recruits were not sufficiently schooled on citizens' legal rights. He also reported that the screening element of time did not keep two violence-prone youths from being graduated. Cordts charged that they were allowed to become Guardian Angels because the new Chicago chapter needed all the members it could get.

Once the requirements have been satisfied, the individual chapters enjoy considerable independence. They may accept financial contributions from community organizations and private citizens, as long as they clear them with Curtis Sliwa in New York. They may make their own arrangements with local government agencies. In most cases, Guardian Angels carry some sort of official identification cards. In only one city, Boston, do they ride the subways and buses free of charge.

In most Angels chapters, members can choose what they wear on patrol, as long as they wear the red beret and T-shirt. But in Philadelphia all Angels on patrol wear camouflage trousers and black boots. And Curtis Sliwa jokes that in Los Angeles the uniform seems to be Pierre Cardin suits.

Where the individual Guardian Angels chapters really differ is in the composition of their membership and in the types of places where they patrol. While nationally, according to Curtis Sliwa, the ethnic makeup of the Guardian Angels is about forty percent Hispanic, thirty percent black, and thirty percent white and Asian, there are many local chapters where the ethnic makeup differs from the average. In New York City the vast majority are black and Hispanic. In Newark, New Jersey, they are mostly black. In Boston many are Jewish. And in Los Angeles, according to Curtis Sliwa, "I was astounded to see blond-haired, blue-eyed boys drive up in cars with surfboards, park and go out on patrol."

Guardian Angels recruits, even if they were from the ghetto, were "good kids to begin with," as a reporter from the Detroit *News* put it. The majority have been class officers, members of sports teams, active in the Boy Scouts and community organizations, and are capable of resisting the lure of crime and the streets. As the organization has grown, it has continued to attract recruits with similar personalities and character. But new recruits tend to be older, nationwide. In three years, the average age has risen from seventeen to twenty-two, and among the new Angels there has been a steadily-increasing number of middle-class, college-educated people. Dallas Dixon, who organized the Angels chapter in Trenton, New Jersey, in the late winter of 1981, is a lawyer, and he was twenty-nine at the time. There are even senior-citizen Angels in some places, for although the minimum age for membership in the organization is sixteen, there is no maximum age. As of December 1981 there was a seventy-two-year-old Angel in Albuquerque, New Mexico, a seventy-year-old in Houston, and a sixty-eight-year-old in Cleveland. They did not go out on patrol—instead, they answered telephones at headquarters. But they were involved.

When an organization that started with teenagers patrolling subways begins branching out to cities where there are no subways, then the areas of patrol change. In the beginning, when the Guardian Angels were a New York City phenomenon associated primarily with that city's subways, it was easy for officials of other cities to dismiss them. In Atlanta, officials said, "We have no subways, so we don't need Guardian Angels." But a city without subways is not a city without crime. Even when they were still just a New York City group, the Guardian Angels quickly branched out, extending their patrols beyond the subways. They set up patrols in Bryant Park (behind the New York Public Library) where drug dealing flourished, and in other parks around the city. So it involved no major change of purpose when the organization moved into other cities. In Los Angeles, Guardian Angels organized bus patrols, and in suburbs around the city, Angels concentrated on house break-ins and assaults in shopping malls. On New Year's Day 1982, Angels even patrolled the route of the Tournament of Roses Parade. In San Francisco, the target areas were Market Street, Telegraph Hill, North Beach, and Fisherman's Wharf. In Boston, where Guardian Angels first started patrolling Boston Commons and the business and theater districts, they have taken on new assignments, such as rebuilding a demolished community center in the Roxbury section.

Although the chief function of the Guardian Angels remains crime prevention, Curtis Sliwa encourages the efforts of other chapters to expand their volunteer activities. After all, the purpose is community involvement in the things that affect the life of the community.

Eventually, Curtis Sliwa would like to see Guardian Angels engaged in many kinds of helping activities. But while his organization was still young he felt that the major concentration should be on the major problem—crime.

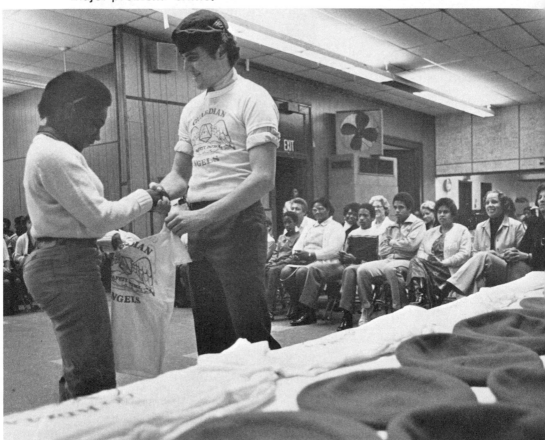

Graduation ceremony of Guardian Angels recruits in New Orleans.—*Laura Elliott*

# How Far Can the
# Wings Stretch?

In just three years, Curtis Sliwa's idea for a citizen crime patrol had become an active reality called the Guardian Angels. They were famous not just in New York City where they began, but all across the country. According to Curtis, people in cities in Europe, Asia, and South America had also asked him for help in starting similar groups. By early 1983, the Guardian Angels claimed 3,000 members in forty cities across the U.S. and extending into Canada.

It is difficult to prove or disprove statistics like these, and one of the complaints government officials have about the Guardian Angels is that their statistics are inaccurate. These officials charge that Curtis Sliwa tends to inflate statistics. For example, when the New York City Police Department began to run records checks on the Angels, Sliwa was claiming a membership of 700 in New York, but only about 550 names were submitted to the Police Department. Sliwa claimed that the New York Guardian Angels had made 158 citizens' arrests as of December 1981, but the Police Department claimed that the Angels had not made a single arrest for a serious crime (a felony).

But Sliwa is not bothered by arguments about conflicting statistics. He points out that from the beginning his main purpose has been to prevent crime. There is no way to measure the number of crimes that were not committed because of the presence of the Guardian Angels. Officials who disapprove of the Angels say that statistics on actual crimes committed do not change as a result of the presence of the Angels. If the Angels were really preventing crimes, say these officials, the number of crimes committed ought to drop.

But in a big city where there are hundreds of crimes committed every day, it would take a huge force of crime preventers to make a difference in the overall crime statistics. Also, statistics can be easily manipulated down as well as up in order to present a certain impression. It is sometimes charged that police deflate or underreport crime figures so it will look as if they are doing a better job than they really are.

Arrest and crime figures do not give the real story. People who tend to look favorably on the Guardian Angels are quick to point this out. Supporters of the Angels include a slowly increasing number of police officials. The New York City Police Department stated for the record that the Guardian Angels did help prevent crime, and in late 1981, the department renewed its first six-month agreement with the Angels. By the early spring of 1982, Sliwa and the New York City Police Department had agreed on a minimal program of formal training: each Guardian Angel received four and one-half hours of police training, including instruction on the legalities of citizens' arrests.

Evidence that the Guardian Angels do prevent crime must necessarily rest on individual reports. There are many. In the fall of 1981 a reporter and a photographer from the Detroit *News* spent four days in New York with the Angels. Curtis Sliwa was organizing an Angels chapter in Detroit, and the city's mayor and police officials were strongly against it. The reporter and photographer wanted to see for themselves the work of the Guardian Angels. They accompanied several groups on patrol.

On one patrol, fourteen Angels were on an uptown Manhattan train, fanning out through the cars as is their custom. Wrote reporter Bill Dunn, "As the train roars uptown, an Angel, who wears a picture of Christ on his backpack because it 'makes me feel safer,' gives a hand signal that brings other Angels running to his car. Three toughs have been talking about the expensive cameras hanging around the neck of another passenger. It might be a mugging in the making; it might not. The arriving Angels say nothing but let themselves be seen. At the next stop the toughs get off the train. It's an example of what many, including some cops, view as the Angels' major value: preventing crimes before they happen simply by their presence, which makes thugs think twice before causing trouble."

Now that there is a chapter in Detroit, Mayor Coleman Young no longer charges that the Angels in that city are a bunch of New Yorkers. And in Washington, D.C., officials there no longer need worry that New York Angels are taking the airline shuttle in every night to patrol the capital. They have accepted that idea that people in their own localities are willing to volunteer for anticrime patrols. But there are many police officers and public officials who remain unconvinced and who still have serious reservations about the Guardian Angels.

The shooting of Guardian Angel Frank Melvin in Newark proves, in the opinion of many law-enforcement people, that tragedy may result when two different groups—the police and the Angels—consider themselves responsible for preventing crime. Houston law-enforcement officials believe that interference by the Guardian Angels can increase the chances for tragedy. They cite an incident that took place in that Texas city in late 1981. An Angels patrol came upon a street fight between two men. One of the men had a gun, and it went off as the Angels tried to restrain him. Although no one was hurt, the police speculated that the shot might have been avoided if the Angels had not gotten themselves involved.

There are private citizens, too, who worry that the Guardian

Angels will turn into a "full-fledged vigilante effort," as one writer to the editor of *The New York Times* put it.

But there are, as has been said, public officials who support the Guardian Angels. And when it comes to private citizens, for every one who worries about the Guardian Angels there are many more who welcome them. Bill Dunn of the Detroit *News* and others who have accompanied the Angels on patrol have reported that people often went right up to the Angels and thanked them for just being there. The Angels are trained not to display emotion while on patrol and are also concerned about keeping up their "macho" image. They simply nod when they receive such compliments, but it is hard not to see the pleasure they feel. So often they are minority youth who are used to being regarded suspiciously by society, especially by adults. Of the adults, the most suspicious have always been the senior citizens, and yet it is senior citizens who seem to welcome the Angels most.

Curtis Sliwa talks a lot about senior citizens. The fact that he was so close to his grandparents when he was young is important to him. When he speaks about the future of the Guardian Angels, he talks about having "a Guardian Angel in every neighborhood," not just to patrol the subways and buses and streets, but to escort senior citizens when they go out shopping and to respond to calls from senior citizens who need help. "I feel we really owe the senior citizens something," says Sliwa, "a payback for the lifestyle we are able to live today."

Lisa Sliwa, like her husband, sees the Guardian Angels getting bigger and more influential in the future and fulfilling the promises of organizations like the Peace Corps and Vista. These organizations were also founded on the idea of individual action and volunteerism, but they failed to attract enough people with the kind of leadership necessary to make them grow.

Leadership is very important to any group effort. Most of the major people's movements in history have depended on strong leaders. That is not to say that the Guardian Angels rank with the important people's movements of the past—at least they do not yet—but it is possible that one day there might be a Guardian Angel in every neighborhood. The idea that people must fight back against the criminals who are trying to take over their neighborhoods and their lives is an idea whose time has come. But history shows that major movements are not just the result of ideas, but of people's willingness to act on those ideas.

Curtis Sliwa and his wife Lisa have proved that they are willing to act on their ideas. They have proved, too, that they have the ability to inspire others to follow them. But in order for any movement to really expand and grow, there need to be more than just one or two people with the power to make decisions. As of this writing, that hasn't happened in the Guardian Angels. Although Curtis Sliwa had begun to delegate responsibility to Lisa, leadership of the Angels still lay so totally with the Sliwas that when they were both in Washington, D.C., for the march to protest the killing of Frank Melvin, Angels patrols in New York were temporarily suspended by Sliwa. Naturally, many New York Angels, particularly the patrol leaders, were furious.

Today, several years after the first patrol of the Magnificent Thirteen, both Curtis Sliwa and his organization face a crossroads. It is not just around the bend, necessarily, but down the road it is pretty much inevitable. How long can Curtis Sliwa go on wearing a white T-shirt and a red beret? How long can he resist the commercial lures that are being dangled in front of him? Every day he is getting requests to endorse, as he once put it, "Angel guard systems. Angel underwear." Then there are the book and movie offers, and the suggestions from supporters that he run for public office. All Curtis Sliwa has said is, "I have gotten a great sense of self-fulfillment from the Angels. . . I don't know if I'll be doing what I'm doing for the rest of my life. This right now is my whole life."

But what if the Guardian Angels organization were to cease being Curtis Sliwa's whole life? Could the group survive without him? "I really believe right will triumph," he has said. "I have faith in people. When given the proper motivation and guidance, they will pick up the ball and run with it. It can work."

# Index